THE CHURCH
OF THE LOVE
OF THE WORLD

First published in 2022 by
The Dedalus Press
13 Moyclare Road
Baldoyle
Dublin D13 K1C2
Ireland

www.dedaluspress.com

ISBN 978-1-910251-96-6 (paperback)
ISBN 978-1-910251-97-3 (hardback)

Dedalus Press titles are available in Ireland
from Argosy Books (www.argosybooks.ie) and in the UK
from Inpress Books (www.inpressbooks.co.uk)

Design and typesetting: Pat Boran
Cover image: stockcam/iStockPhoto.com

The Dedalus Press receives financial assistance from
The Arts Council / An Chomhairle Ealaíon.

THE CHURCH
OF THE LOVE
OF THE WORLD

GRACE WELLS

DEDALUS PRESS

ACKNOWLEDGEMENTS

Thanks are due to the editors of the following magazines and periodicals in which some of these poems, or versions of them, first appeared:

Magma, Seed Journal, The Temenos Academy Review, The Stranger Times, Trasna, Of Claws and Hooves and Meadows (Poetry Ireland in partnership with UCD School of Veterinary Medicine).

And to the editors of RTÉ's programmes *Sunday Miscellany, Arena* and *Poetry File* where some of these poems were first broadcast.

The author would also like to extend her sincere gratitude to The Arts Council / An Chomhairle Ealaíon for a Literature Bursary in 2021, and a Professional Development Award in 2020 which supported the completion of this manuscript.

Sincere thanks to Clare County Council Arts Office for the provision of a 2021 Artist's Bursary. And to both Poetry Ireland and Clare County Council Arts Office for the creation of the Poetry Town 2021 project, for which the author was Poet Laureate for Ennistymon.

Large thanks also go to the organisers of the Cashel Arts Festival 2019, for whom the author curated the project 'Poetry on the Rock', a celebration of The Rock of Cashel through poetry. Some of the poems created for that project, first published in the anthology *Stone on Stone,* appear here.

Thank you also to The Junction Festival, Clonmel, which first broadcast 'Leaving Glenaskeogh'.

Much of this work would not exist without the kindness and support of Manuela Palacios-Gonzales, Pat Boran, Lani O'Hanlon, Cathy Fitzgerald, James Harpur, Sean Lysaght, Mark Granier, Mark Roper and Keith Payne.

A number of these poems also exist as poetry-films, and can be viewed at *www.gracewellslittlesanctuary.com.*

Contents

≋

⤴

what the body holds

⤴

psalm

⤴

in wonder and in grief

⤴

For Holly

This is how I want the poems to be:
trembling with light, coarse with earth,
murmuring with waters and with wind.

—Eugénio de Andrade

Vestige

Things being so urgent, when you
open a book its leaves should take you
back to the forest they came from,

the creak of beech, the wind-restless pine;
between these covers a scent of resin and loam.

A book's spine like the trunk of a tree to lean into,
the pulp of its paper, a fine mesh of twig and sky.

Each word on the page so verdant, viridian
that you soften into moss, and strengthen
into the stubborn protective root of briar.

Type and ink like the small handiwork of ant,
the quiet labour of beetle and wasp
mending the world between endpapers

in such a deep entangling way
as to make you part of the woodland,
embowered, arboreal, sylvan.

We Speak on the Out Breath

At the writers' festival several days go by
without leaf or flower.
No glimpse of river, no shriek of white gull.

At the writers' festival few speak of
the more-than-human world,
as if our thinking has been tamed.

So forgive my urge to slink a vixen
through the bars of our cage;

forgive my desire to show deer
where our wire sags
and our boundary can be breached.

Like a woman pulling curtains against
the night, I want to draw
a glade of trees around us,

and coax honey-suckle across this ceiling;
let these walls become a waterfall
to drown the traffic from the street.

We might sit then in the fading light,
sit as the Quakers do, waiting
for a spirit to move our tongues.

*Let the words you speak be worthy
of the silence you break*, a woman once
said in my hearing and I wished she hadn't,

it was hard enough anyway to know
what to say, how not to sound like the canary
in my brain cheeping its constant alarm.

Perhaps it's too late to talk of the animals,
to remember the way elephants curl their
trunks to caress the bones of their dead.

I was hoping this poem would be
a song-bird that could land on your open palm,
but the small thud we didn't hear

when we were so busy listening to the sound
of our own thoughts, was the small-winged body
of nature breaking against glass.

It's a hurt bird we carry in our hands,
my friends wake with its feathers in their mouths.

The next breath any of us draw will not
descend from up on high
but has risen from the ground beneath our feet,

what enters our lungs comes now
from bush and briar and yellow whin,

from each leaf on every tree in the shrinking forest
of the Southern Hemisphere,

so how can I not speak of growing-things,
the lone cowslip in the ditch, the last orchid in the parish,
the latest disappearance from disease or carelessness –

which reminds me of the black car-battery someone
has tossed in the harbour at Dungarvan, its acid
leaching a toxic-drip into the veins of our intelligent web.

When we speak, we speak on the out-breath,
but must first draw in the fine threads of this Earth.

Whatever we speak of now,
we will need to be like blades of prairie grass
that bend in the wind of what's coming.

Perhaps the only sensible thing would be
to howl, the way Europe's last
twelve-thousand wolves are surely howling – a sound

somewhere between grief and battle-cry,
the tribes of us in this together, tasked
to heed Emerson, and *Advance.*

> *Advance upon chaos and the dark.*

and all the winds said leave

Beach Clean

Like women in the fields gathering grain, we are
bent over in the river-mouth harvesting plastic:

fishing-net, bottle tops, baling twine, gun cartridges,
a flower pot, a zip from a windcheater, a child's balloon.

And worst is that each time we lift a clump of sea-weed,
twenty or thirty minute fragments of plastic loosen
and float off downriver to the waiting tide.

And I'm crying. Not wanting the other volunteers to see,
crying, not for the quantity of plastic we're collecting,

but because I've finally given-up on
the man I've loved for more than a year.
Turns out he's more troubled than I thought.

And I'm weeping because it seems
this is all I've ever known of love,

but I carry on harvesting plastic: turquoise, scarlet, pink.
Things I've no idea what they once were, sniffing

and trying not to cry, although what else should you do
when you've harvested enough fishing-net to catch

a dolphin, and one of the other volunteers has already
told you how many dolphins wash up dead each year.

I put their image in my sack, along with the carcass
of a gull I find, its throat strangled by orange twine.

In the poor bird goes among the cigarette butts,
cellophane and other foul-smelling things.

And I carry on with my task, stooped in the river water,
human enough to weep for the oceans,

      creature enough to howl for her mate.

Leaving Glenaskeogh

All through the cold months the storms
blew in wuthering their same song:
a woman who has lost her dream, has lost her way.

Clearly someone, taking things apart
had put the pieces back together wrong,

and what with the isolation
and the storms that snowed me in,

I was alone in ways I'd never been –
and no longer able for such loneliness.

And all the winds said: *Leave,*
a woman who has lost her dream, has lost her way.

But how to extract yourself from the land
when its spring-water runs in your veins,

and your lungs are the pale lichens
that grow in the larch trees.

When to leave would be to leave down
a wildflower meadow,
and the freedom of pine-woods,

and the wild heather-moors of a mountain
you have come to consider your own.

How to leave the hare, the fox, the badger?
How to part with the hooded-crows that
warned you of danger?

To leave would be to sever yourself
from seasons of hawthorn,
from the blossom and berry on the elder and sloe.

To leave would send your feral self to live beneath
the orange of street-lamps, by the clock of sirens.

To leave would end a good marriage,
for that acre at Glenaskeogh had seen me
in all my moods, and never judged,

it understood the woman in me –
let me see her for myself.

And if we were some kind of lovers,
our betrothal was the ground itself –

the way that sometimes of an evening, the acre
would unfurl a fabric of scents. An intoxication.

To leave would be to abandon my every precious thing.
But a woman who has lost her dream, has lost her way,

and a place doesn't just nurture a person.
I'd like to say the land was ever kind,
but the field was a field after all,

nettles took over, gorse covered the hill,
briars twisted me the way ivy trusses trees –

billhook and blade turning me into a man
until the girl in me had all but waned.

I was only ever a pair of arms, trying to
raise my family, earn a living, write my books.

But it was when I was pulling myself out
of Glenaskeogh that I saw I'd written nothing at all –

squandered *my whole possession*,
all the song-birds, the grasses, all the small
whispers of wren and violet.

Nothing so intimate as place.

For fifteen years a kestrel watched over me –
I loved her with all of my heart.

For so long they were our ark, now we must be theirs

'From the beginning of the world, the creatures and plants were our lifeboat that got us to where we are now. Now we must be a lifeboat for them.'
—Robin Wall Kimmerer

So I take down the children's old ark,
paint-chipped and dusty, its animals lost
or strewn in a jumbled heap.

I paint the belly of the ark gold
because for so long they were our ark
and now we must be theirs,

so I make space for the species in the cabin,
space for the native black-willow dying
on the shores of the Kentucky river.

Space for the river itself. I colour the hull
of the boat sky-blue to repair the cloak of
our atmosphere, because if the sky isn't our ark,

I don't know what is. I paint the waves of our
rising seas, and work in cold greens and greys
to cool the oceans, I use alkali to balance their acid,

and leave out the pollutants and plastics,
the fish-hooks and net, and I call to the birds
that it's safe to nest on this roof,

the threatened swallows, the last storks, the precious owls.
From their hutches, I release the factory-farmed hens,
the industrialised ducks, and the Christmas turkeys.

Then I gather up the wooden animals my children
played with years ago before they left for the city.

Of all the mammals on the globe, only four percent
are free, the rest we keep for our own purposes,

so I hold the creatures gently while I paint their limbs,
and I say to them, *for so long you were our ark,*
now we must be yours: the lion, the crocodile,
the elephants, the giraffes.

Two by two I give them back their names
and their dignity. I return them to the wild.

Charm bracelet

'Hibernia' meant the land of eternal winter

And me being me, I go all over Cashel's Rock
looking for signs of nature – clergy and kings not
having half the potency of meadow flowers.

I'm curious about the plants they used for ale,
how honey became mead; how rosemary
and sage made metheglins that Pepys said
Could stupefy, and keep a humming in the brain.

I want to know which strewing herbs they
tossed on floors, pennyroyal against ticks,
hyssop, fleabane, rue for the churches,
mint and chamomile to sweeten air.

The higher you build, the closer you come to heaven
the guide said, but I bent low to the ferns
in the walls, searching the cracks of history
for any clue – wattle marks in the plaster,

a sandstone bull with wings, an eagle feathered
with granite diamonds like the scales of a fish.
It was like following a trail of crumbs, nature
banished to mere decoration;

ornament on the furniture in the museum:
wooden acorns, an oaken swathe of foliage,
an eight-petalled rose. But I kept on looking
stringing a catechism, like collecting charms for

a bracelet: a frieze of grapes on a limestone vine,
a long-stemmed lily whose petals strained
towards God, whose sepals spiraled
back to the good Earth.

It is hard to find her intricacies within the grandeur,
but nonetheless she is there –
the feminine, lifting her lovely head.

Each time I pass the brothel

another mature woman in black leather and red lipstick
is stood at the door looking out, indifferent to
the smile I offer. Only days since I'd read Shaw:

how the difference *between a flower girl and a lady*
is not the way she behaves, but how she's treated.

In jest my latest lover had called me *a woman of easy virtue* –
and my litany of romantic disasters proved his phrase true.

There but for the grace of God, I say passing the whores,
passing the can-drinkers urinating in the street,

passing the man with the blonde beard and long hair
who looks like Jesus but talks aloud to himself,

jabbing his finger, shaking his perfect head, while the city
turns and ignores him. Leaving me to puzzle

how anyone so beautiful could be so troubled? Grateful
that my own worst complaint has been loneliness.

In the light of day, in a world submerged beneath child-porn
and the traffic of women, loneliness seems like a blessing,

so I lift myself up, as *God* has so often lifted me,
I speak to all the earlier versions of myself that
couldn't sleep and lived in fear; one day, I want to tell you,

you will walk through the streets of Vigo with
a bag of peaches under your arm,
their comforting weight the steady measure of your wealth.

Among Tourists the Eco-Poet Feels Her Myth

There is a graceful symmetry to
the elderly Indian couple

whose arms and hands are poised
to shore up Pisa's tower in its lean.

They keep their hold as temple-dancers might,
only the hem of her sari lifts on the breeze.

Around them mill chattering
delegates from every nation,

a thicket of selfie-sticks beams
persona across our fragile globe.

On the lawn, an artist has sprawled
a marble-winged angel, fallen –
lovely and believable.

But I pass through the crowded piazza
in the long skirts of murderous thought,

like Medea, or Clytemnestra,
nothing but disdain and blame,
and blood on my hands.

Farewell

When I left, I turned back to look –
fearing it might be for the last time.

It was May, evening, everything lush green,
her courtyards a haze of blue forget-me-not.

We hugged goodbye, and I clung to her –
she was the same age as my mother,
and I, as old as her daughter.

For whatever reason, she had taken me to her heart –
perhaps because hers was a large heart,

or perhaps it was because we both understood
something of the state of our precious Earth.

I shouldn't have let her pour all that wine,
but we were drinking to drown out sorrow.

What was I holding in that last embrace?
All her love. All her travels in a once-world.

Tree Fell

That summer, while I waited
for the house to sell,
they came for the pine-forest.

The loggers moved up the hill
with their screaming saws,

unaware they were tearing down
my shelter, destroying
what had been my church.

Resin on my palms I walked
through the last of the wood,

putting my hands to each trunk,
whispering, *I'm sorry, I'm sorry*,

thanking each of them,
saying goodbye.

Then, with the machines' roar
at my back,

I did the only thing left to me,
I took off my dress,
and walked naked among the trees.

The Years of My Mothering

'If only, most lovely of all, I yield myself and am borrowed
by the fine, fine wind that takes its course through the chaos of the world'
—D.H. Lawrence

The Rock was ever in the background, steady
and dependable as my view of the Commeraghs,

as much a part of Tipperary as the river Suir
and the Galtee mountains, and the Devil's bit.

Iconic, it carried all the splendour and pomp
of male history, iconic, it meant Ireland, invasion,
colonization, and patriarchal faith. So mostly

I ignored the Rock, except when visitors came,
and I had to show them round, a stiff breeze blowing,
and tea afterwards by the fire in the Cashel Palace Hotel.

But it was local see, local as standing on the side of
a GAA pitch with your son playing, and the rain lashing down,
local as the blue and gold of the Tipperary flag,

local as the green and white of the Grangemockler
jersey Michael Hogan was shot in on
that first Bloody Sunday up in Croke Park.

The Rock was local as the sudden scent of turf smoke in
September, local as the Golden Vale, and Golden itself,
and Holycross, Killanaule, Ballinure, Fethard –

equine country with all the nobility of the Irish horse,
someone telling me a horse's heart weighs ten times
that of a man's. And it was those hearts we lived among,

for it was in the shelter of the Rock that I spent
the years of my mothering. So, if like the salmon

my children are ever called back to their
spawning grounds, this is where they will come.

Sometimes I ask myself, what did I give them with
my threadbare poet's life –

but what they breathed was the clean air of
the heather moors of Sliabh na mBan,
and what they drank was clear spring water,

they grew up in the small lanes of Tipperary,
with the skeagh and the hawthorn,

and when I think of those years it is always
May or June, the white of cow-parsley
along the ditches, the chestnut-trees in bloom.

If I gave them anything, it was these neighbours,
these friends, these fields like a cloak to their backs,

it was the boughs of these trees they climbed
in their hand-me-downs, and all the time the Rock

was there, like the hub
of the wheel our lives turned around,

so when you came on it suddenly, cresting a hill,
there it was crowning the horizon,
and you didn't think of history, or High Kings,

you only knew what *belonging* meant,
how it was to feel yourself at home.

Innumerate contributors

'Air is nothing but a mixture of a variety of gasses'
—Lenntech Industries

Each seed-head, each blossom offers
perfume, colour, light.

The ferns uncoil in the woods,
the leaves unfurl on the trees,
the fabric of the air changes,

place like breath is made
of innumerate stitches,

small threads of pine needle,
the sticky brown tips on the chestnut tree,
the minute red silks of scarlet pimpernel.

And above them, airborne, the translucencies,
insect wing, butterfly, moth,
the petal-light grades of fragility.

And water doing what water does –
clearing, cleansing, cooling the air.

The day fading, the first star coming out.
I love you, evening, I said.
I love you, I said to the mountain, to the meadow.

Such a bittersweet, impossible parting.

to bend like prarie grass

Grass

Grass, I've been watching you,
so slow to turn from winter to spring,

then growth green and low,
pushing up your language
of spikelet and seed-head,

soft, blowsy, tufted,
florets and anthers and awns.

A plenitude. A beatitude.
Some old religious word
for abundance and beauty combined,

but nothing lofty,
just grass,

fescue, scutch, timothy,
dog's tail, fox tail,
hard-grass, hair-grass, heath.

Where grain begins.
Where it all begins,

down in the grass.

She Gathers the Wild Grasses

'Mainly we were hungry to convert everything to profit.
Still nomads – still strangers
To our whole possession.'
—Ted Hughes, 'Daffodils'

'To take up one hundred grasses is to take up yourself'
—Eihei Dogen

At first I arrange them in an earthen jug –
one of every grass
that grows along the road to Panicale.

Something in their form, their green or grain,
invites a quickening, kernel-deep,

and I remember how it was women
who gathering the first grasses

and scattering their seed,
became the earliest farmers –

inventing an agriculture
that brought the nomadic tribes
to rest.

In the stone house at Panicale,
beneath its terracotta roof,
with doors and windows open,

we flow between rooms on tides
of birdsong, neither outside nor entirely in.

The walls our shelter, but porous,
permeable to the lift of wings,
to every small beak and throat,

and church-bells across the hill,
announcing each swallow-stitched hour.

　　　　　　　　⤸

There are tall daisies
in the meadow beneath the house,

golden trefoil, and a tendril weave
of campion, sweetpea, and purple vetch.

There are twelve kinds of orchid,
and countless other flowers I cannot name,

but still I reach for grass.

　　　　　　　　⤸

And dusk is not so much the fade of light,
but the wake and call of tawny owls.

From the terrace, we drift our gaze
across valleys of endless-seeming trees,

and trace the erratic dart and loop of bats
dissolving in the darkening sky.

Pipistrelles, Mark names them,
and he recently returned from watching

whales in the San Ignacio lagoon, says
it's the wild creatures that give me shelter.

Sean leaves our evening chatter –
descends the stone stairs
towards the olive grove.

How long before he re-emerges
through the fallen night

and leads us after him
like children, to see the fireflies.

Theirs is a dance
of tiny miraculous lights,

of minute torches
searching meadow-grass,

a theatre we stand in ovation for,
transfixed.

I lay the different grasses
along a page of my notebook,

each green stalk with its differing spike,
or soft-branched panicle.

An assemblage of meadow-art,
arranged on white paper

with the hope that seed or form will gift
me meaning, sane and nourishing as grain.

Grass 1: Italian rye, its stem stiff as wire,
its spike a plain, concise head –

an inflorescence of thin seeds
tight as chain-mail

which suggests all our inventions
are mere copies from nature's archetype.

And I remember the fragments
I've seen of early temples

how the Goddess
held a sheath of wheat,

and her sanctuaries
were furnished

with a quern-stone for grinding,
and a hearth for baking,

and bread was sacrament.

Grass 2: Anisantha, with a shine to its pink casings,
so that light and green and mauve turn

like a mobile above a baby's cot
whispering a prayer of grass.

They lure me in the grasses –
fascinators.
Textured, tactile.

Their green hairs – their awns – so fine
you'd think they'd fray
or fail in wind and rain,

and yet they have
the tensile strength
to withstand gale,

the presence to quieten me.

Grass 3: Floating Sweet Grass with long, thin
seed-heads – long glumes – that might once
have given us the measure of an inch.

Still nomads, Hughes wrote,
still strangers to our whole possession.

Is it that we skim
the surface of this Earth

rootless as stones skimmed
across the surface of a lake –

our lives in flight.

If I reach for grass,
is it to work a snare?

As if my woman's hand could
bring our tribes to rest,

and let the wild grasses
offer up another agriculture –

white-rooted, rhizomed, mycorrhizal,
all things in their connection.

It is bread I love when I travel.
How place gives up its different loaf.

Focaccia from Liguria,
Tuscan bread made without salt.

An alphabet of breads, local as Waterford's
soft *blaa*, and across the Comeragh mountains,
trays of *grinders* in Clonmel.

I've had the luck to live
loaf by loaf,

to weigh out flour
and prove my own dough –

something forever illiterate
and welcome
in signing each crust with my mark.

Grass 4: Creeping Soft-grass, which begins
silken, tufted, packed,

only to dive into the abandon of branches –
the mimic of a minute, rose-coloured tree.

Give us this day our daily bread,
and forgive us our trespasses
as we forgive those who trespass against us.

When we soaked our wheat in toxins,
it was not without consequence,

I watched my daughter crumple up in pain,
cry out as her belly cramped

until we understood
the effects of glyphosate.

We shopped then
for other nation's grains:
quinoa, chia, amaranth.

And there were few reports of how
the prices of those staples rose,

the hunger and civil unrest,
how one thing could lead to
another half a world away –

poison in our fields, and batons
coming down on women and children.

Grass 5: An ear of wild barley,
four-sided.

Awns thick as a fox's tail
hiding a central axis of seed

ready to issue north,
east, south and west,

like a compass-grass
directing us nowhere

but here, here, here.

No doubt they sew me to life
or tack me at least,

the way my sister the dressmaker
fixed cloth with a loose-stitched hem.

I harvest the wild grasses
as I harvest the scattered seeds of myself.

If I love the grasses
it is because they are humble, forgotten,

and yet their necks bend
not in shame, but elegance.

Grass 6: Timothy, with hairs thinner
than eyelash, soft as down,
allowing the seed-head seem almost mammal.

All year I've listened to
the whispered worry of my friend

whose child was born with a damaged heart,
her baby in and out of surgery ever since.

She says in the cardiac ward of the children's hospital
you can read why babies come with faulted hearts,

and top of the reasons is
their mother's proximity to farmland.

Mothers, the report says, *share
their chemical load with the fetus.*

*One study found pregnant women
could come into contact
with 248 individual farm-chemicals.*

Grass 7: which is a kind of oat, almost like
a fishing-rod bowed with a dozen fork-tailed fish,

their minute seed-heads leaf-wrapped
like small cobs of corn,

and pendulous, designed as if to capture
always this word, this delicate *trembling*.

For the longest time I had
these suspicions.

I said if we've grown intolerant,
what of the creatures?

What's happening to the fieldmice,
the voles, the hares?

It's the woman from Liscannor
who tells me about the hedgehog
she finds bewildered on the road.

How her vet says it's all he sees nowadays,
wild animals with tumors and the like.

Our last night at Panicale I sleep badly,
in and out of dreams, concerned with an
early departure, and un-ready to leave.

Is it that we skim the surface of this Earth
still nomads, still strangers to our whole possession?

Returning sleep-eyed from the bathroom
I find in the darkness of my room
a firefly winking her intermittent light.

At five the birds begin to sing again
I get up and walk into their sound.

47

It is a lifetime's work
this opening to grace.

At length the heart so open
tears pour forth at the slightest thing,

at the sight of
pollen drifted to a notebook's page.

⤳

If there is a last thing to be said,
let it be for the curlews

who make their nests in meadow grass,
letting long stems encircle eggs.

All May I walked the beach at Kilmacreehy,
a dozen of our last curlews
flew about my head.

When I spoke to them, what could I say?
This is who we've become, I owned –

the kind of people who
wouldn't grant you so much land
as the round space of an old cob-loaf.

All through May I walked the sand at Kilmacreehy,
a dozen curlews encircling my thoughts.

In June, returned from Italy, they had disappeared.

⤳

When I close my eyes,
the fireflies of Panicale

dance behind my lids,
the owls announce evening on the air.

And they not knowing
how the armies of progress advance.

In such blessed pockets of place
may all continue as it ever was,
and the church bells toll *sanctuary*.

ocean, cliff and tide

The Day I Settled in Ennistymon

was the day Michael suddenly drove over from Golden,
bringing the sun with him, chasing off the long winter of
my being a stranger, everything unfamiliar, even myself.

It turned out he'd lived in the town as a boy, for five sweet
years when his father ran the bank. We shared tea on
the café-terrace overlooking the cascades, and Michael said

how the building was once the post-office, and a man
who hunted rabbits sold the postmistress her own dead cat.
And when I told him that couldn't be true, he said maybe

it was only a story. He had lots of stories – about the fellow
with a cart who collected bones from all the butchers and tipped
offal from his gate into the cascades, which led the eels

to wait in the pools below, and boys like Michael to
gather on the rocks, *Big conger eels that came thrashing after you,*
and you only six years old, with no way to kill them, but your penknife.

In the spring light we walked through the town, Michael saying
how once he could have gone in any door, as the bank-manager's son
he'd been welcome in every house. And as if that hadn't changed,

he took liberties with alleys and back-yards, to show me where pigs
were once kept and killed, to reveal the town's secrets. Up Churchill
we went, to where the rough boys had had their gang. And round

his old school where no teacher ever laid a hand on him, though
every other child got clattered. Side-by-side we walked beneath
his old rooms in the bank, him telling me about his Ennistymon,

and my talk of the present day, the cafés and bookshops, the surfers
and artists, the re-wilders and organic-growers, the two of us weaving
a plait of two towns. Then we followed the Inagh into the woods,

up Tattens, where the bluebells were coming, the ferns uncurling.
In the trees were the first green leaves of a new beginning, Michael
still talking, telling me story after story,

                              until he had brought me home.

Sea Swimmers

The leaves turn yellow, the blackberries ripen
and folk come from town with baskets,

children with purpled fingers catch
at sycamore keys whirling down.

And day after day the women keep on swimming
elongating summer, stretching its sweetness,

streeling out its days, to return like seals to the rocks at Clahane,
the swimming hole at Whitestrand, and the beach at Lahinch,

to plunge themselves into water and sky,
to shiver afterwards in the raw air.

Eking out summer even as October
fades into November's dark,

they are quivering wet,
clinging on like the last leaves,

as if the women of the West were amphibious,
built for more than just the gravity of land.

Until even they must at last surrender,
and swim back upriver to the winter hearth.

Naiad

Here, when rain falls after
the slurry is spread in the fields,

the river runs thick with scum,
the naiad of the Inagh drowns again.

I carry my sorrow to St Brigid's well,
once more take refuge in her plainsong,
Everything tangled shall be unraveled.

Curlew

'*What an unearthly aria that call was. Hearing his voice, a god who had made the curlew would almost instantly want to remake himself as the thing he had made. Universes he couldn't call into being with a human voice he could call into being with the voice of a curlew.*'
—John Moriarty

Above the beach at Kilmacreehy,
ten curlews become eleven curlews

in a small flock of wing and glide
I follow after like a younger child.

Birds possessed of little more than sky –
a sky so blue it turns the waves aquamarine,
and lights the wet sand cobalt-blue,

Liscannor Bay become so sheltering
that I am almost fooled to forget
how the curlews are fading now;

the wings that fly around my head
trace a fragile cusp of life,
the wick of their species is burning low.

So in the way that others sit
at the bedsides of the dying,

I accompany the curlews out
to where their blue sands will surely end,

but each soft step sinks me deeper
into our Earth's embrace,

and when the curlews call,
their song enchants –

lifting me with them,
until I am airborne, feathered, flying.

Dove

for Jazz and Mitch

The dove in my heart flew out,
I'm lonely, she cried circling the room,
flapping a frantic white-feathered flight.

What could I do but release her?
Off she flew down Main Street,
looking in at the windows, searching.

Couples still sleeping,
couples rising unwilling to greet each other,
marriages entrenched in conflict.

I worried for my dove as she tried
to navigate the world.

For the longest time she could find
only resentment and complaint.

Go to Mitch and Jazz's place, I told her.
And off she lifted over the greening fields
to the small cottage at the foot of Moy hill.

There she drank her fill of happiness,
and has not yet returned.

Learning the Hill

Watching the cows on Duffy's hill:
mother and calf, mother and calf

in a lumbering, slow-bellied
drift of weighty grace.

Languor in everything
except jaw and chew.

Dignity in the swish of their long tails,
graceful as the lift and turn of dervish skirts.

One huge pale cow is brindled grey-blue,
a moon-cow, milk-bathed,
and followed by her pale moon calf.

Only the delicate placement of each hoof,
and the sundial of their shadows
measures the morning's slow advance.

My eyes follow their graze across the hill,
calf following cow, calf following cow,
luring me bovine deeper,

until I am stilled enough
to see grass, cow, milk, moon:
Boann, Boann, Boann,

as if She never left,
was always in and of this place.

Banais Ríghi, the High King Speaks

*'The land is the figure of the great Goddess Anu whom Cormac Mac
Cuilleariáin, King and Bishop of Cashel described as Mater deorurn
hibernorurn, the mother of the gods of the Irish.'*
—Sean Ó Duinn

I have always thought she looked
her loveliest from here.

Here more than anywhere
she gave herself to me –
this ground our bridal bed.

When I married her,
she gave me her intricacies,

apple blossom, birdsong,
the salmon's rainbow breast,

the white swans
and the white geese.

The word *feis* meant
to sleep with the Goddess,
to be permeated by her.

When I married her,
I became the mountains,
I became the forest.

Her soft rain fell
and I grew as grain.
When I married her,

she turned me copper,
gave me the strength of iron.

She crowned me with
the goldcrest's burnished head.

In her embrace I was kingfisher,
turquoise, emerald, amber.

She released me
as falcon on the wing.

The veins in my wrists
became the rivers of the land,

when anything happens to her,
it happens to me.

It is my relationship with the land
which grants me sovereignty –
this ground our bridal bed.

For her it was strewn with
the creamy-white petals
of elderflower, of meadowsweet.

She never left our bedchamber
without an offering for my palm:

acorn, sea-shell, chrysalis, amethyst,
a hazelnut drilled empty
and open by one of her creatures.

And after her leaving,
the room echoed with her –

a steady incantation
Tuath, Tuath, Tuath
meaning people, meaning place.

Lattice

Come, I said to the creatures, nest,
drey, burrow, warren, set.

Come briar, weave a covert for fox.
Come willow, knit an earth for badger.

Grass, grow tall enough for hare's form,
safe enough for the leverets in spring.

Come, I said to the creatures, return,
while I live, you will be safe on this half-acre.

Who have we been with our evictions?
Poor landlords. Drunk squanderers.
We have gambled our fortune.

Burrow neighbouring bolt-hole,
beside rhizome, beneath lair.

Frogspawn to pool. Salmon gilt to the stream.
Eel to the river. Hawk to the hill.

Come home, I called to the species.
Let us build a lattice of shelters close on one another.
Let us restore the matrix of home.

what the body holds

Three Nudes

'All life's grandeur is something with a girl in summer'
—Robert Lowell

Nobody else remembers but I do –
his polaroid experiments in black and white –

taken in Cornwall on an empty beach,
he positioning me, insisting I turn
my head away until shadow hid my face.

So much of that holiday I'd cycled
after him, unable to keep up,
but the two nudes don't reveal that –

just my young self, posed on rocks, light
and granite lending themselves to his art,
they frame me like a pearl.

And though I'd never advocate a girl
expose her body to a lens,

I'm glad I did, for these images are pure demure,
all shoulder, waist and long stretch of leg.

No man ever told me how beautiful I was,
but the nudes say it clear.

And now that my looking-glass reveals
only fading grandeur, I don't regret that day,

nor the lone photograph of myself pregnant,
naked in sunlight against the cottage door,

a cat purring at my ankles.

All the loveliness of woman
with her vast, potent curve of pregnancy.

My daughter curled within,
and never again so safe.

Indigenous

No longer native of anywhere, I sift
archaeologies to feel a root

and find myself in Sussex, a summer child,
visiting Fishbourne and the Roman palace,

learning the experience of mosaic from the floor's
design of dolphin, trident and hoofed sea-mare.

Amphora and tendrils of vine
re-created from minute tiles,

panther, griffin, large-petalled flowers –
the Romans didn't *have* to make mosaic,

but being pagan, I expect they understood
how nature conjures herself from detail.

Leaves build like tesserae to make a tree,
bird is an opus of feather, beak, eye, and more.

Mouseios meant *belonging to the Muses*;
the Romans perceived the ground as art.

I was a child starring at where history began,
not yet knowing how her world was made,

nor of what lay beneath that floor – a Celtic inheritance,
the sacred names and nature of place, a lost linguistics.

And that, lain over an earlier hoard:
bone, flint, woad,
                    and my own dear, indigenous heart.

The limits of my language, are the limits of my world

In the night, soft rain has fallen,
welling up a sweet perfume of leaf and soil.

Weeks without rain, the loam so dry
she will need to get used to tenderness again –

for the first time the new green leaves
feel how it is to be wet.

I have been reading of
the old religions – their appreciation of dew,

how the Chinese Goddess Kwan Qin pours
the dew of mercy over the world each morning.

In Ireland, Brigid's dew is generous,
falls to bless each living thing.

My thoughts flow towards the moisture
a woman secretes when she is aroused;

how the vessels of the vulva
pass fluid through the vaginal wall –
the gateway to pleasure that ushered my children in.

But it has no name this dew
which continues the human world.

I announce that to the wet morning,
the earth releasing her own moistures
as I stand within the scents of petrichor.

Chameleon, inhabit, embody

The valley is terraced,
so to swim in the pool

is to move arms and legs
through aquamarine

while your eyes rest in
the soft branches of olive trees
rooted in the grove below.

Their fine, thin leaves are silver
and a deeper darker green,

an olive haze softened
by silver-grey lichen.

And because I believe
I am in the last years of my life

because I want now
to live as if there were no separation
between myself and nature,

I swim from one olive tree
to another, part of their silver mist,

then back through
clear, blue water,

then out with the last swallow
into the wide evening sky

settling to roost again
in an olive-tree's embrace,

silvered once more
like a chameleon absorbing place.

The Undervalued Linguistics of Compassion

for Pat Boran

It is winter here, sparse comfort, rain
spilling from the gutters, storm worrying the roof.

In the night I dream of becoming a salmon,
an itch to my skin that is the beginning of scales.

Craythur, you say down the phone
and the word contains a world of sympathy.

The soft Midlands fields of your youth accompany
the word over miles, from out of other dark days,
echoing your mother or grandmother in kindness,

to reach me in the savage place I find myself.
Craythur, you say, and coax me back to being human.

What the Body Holds

He's new to me, this healer, so I'm trying to describe
why my left leg does this, my right does that,
the strange sensations in my tissue, but's there's

too much to account for, the story so long,
besides which it's impossible to explain the energies
a woman gathers living in a patriarchal world.

So instead I start gabbling about Cuba, how I've
been following this documentary series with its
several hundred years of images and film:

colonization, revolution, dictatorship,
colonization, revolution, dictatorship,
revolution, dictatorship, and how every photograph,

every film clip is of men: men disembarking from ships,
men firing cannons, men firing guns, men on horses
fighting men with machetes, men in battledress,

men raising the flags of conquering nations,
victorious men hectoring from podiums,
and Zapatistas, and CIA agents trying to oust them,

and men cutting down forests, men spraying fields,
men around board tables, men shaking hands,
sugar-barons, cigar-moguls, oil tycoons,

patricians in arm-chairs, and mafia bosses dangling
the occasional bikini-clad girl. And all of this footage
is intercut with male historians pontificating about Cuba.

None of this should come as any surprise –
I know our history – but somehow, hour after hour,
this documentary series explains the world to me,

and how very brief the era of woman has been.
That's the story my body is holding,
but it doesn't translate into words, so suddenly I'm saying,

See, women are like horses. There's the early years
when we're groomed to gleam like thoroughbreds,
high-heels and make-up – a kind of dressage.

And later if there's pregnancy and birth that's prescribed too,
women lying down like Queen Victoria,
or herded into medical procedures much likes mares.

My mind canters over my years of child-rearing,
the drudgery and repetition, something like a dray-horse
pulling her plough, then switching to the gymkhana at night.

Then I think of growing older, the way doctors say
things like *At your age*, how they consider parts of a woman
no longer necessary, but my mind is vaulting to the day

at the race-course, the gallop of hooves, and how when
the mare fell, the screens were round her in a minute, a vet
with a gun, and she was gone as if she'd never been.

My body holds all of that, and this new healer
he doesn't argue, he seems in his way to understand,

whatever his hands are doing, it's working,
my tensions drop away, I start to hear my health.

Come evening, I watch the last episode about Cuba,
Hugo Chávez who has played such a role
in Cuba's recent story has died from cancer,

Fidel is frail now, and Raúl Castro getting ready to retire,
and the vultures are swarming: Obama, Trump, Biden.

One day they'll look back at our times in the way
I look back at the women of the 'Sixties. They'll say
Such early days, such lives, those women were amazing.

I go among horses, I apologise.

The Third Age

Her young body puddles at her feet,
she steps out of it like casting off a petticoat.

Taller now, she is crossing a stream
the girls may not yet follow.

In the Falls Hotel an elderly woman
offers up a glass of Crème de Menthe,
Go on, try it, do, she says.

And I take the emerald translucence
from her wizened hand, knowing

she is proffering decline,
eccentricity, insignificance,
the infirmities I have always been immune to.

I only sip. How unfamiliar it tastes –
I had expected something displeasing,

am shocked to find it compelling,
dangerous, and so extraordinarily sweet.

Fallow

Currently I'm not selling anything,
I've nothing to sell.

I'm letting myself lie fallow.
I'm running to seed.

What I need is a month of Sundays,
a year of them.

Like a well not drawn from
until water refills.

Like a sacred cow,
not driven.

I'm not asking anything
of this ground.

I want the shiver of quaking grass within me,
nothing more.

If there's mud on my shoes,
or wisps of straw in my hair,
that's good.

Mostly I'm just interested
in loving the world.

The last bird of evening is singing within me.
She's all I wish to hear.

psalm

An account of that year in fragments

At the kitchen table, in her fur-grey dressing-gown
like a seal-woman, Lani leads me through
small Feldenkrais movements.

Afterwards she says, *Now*
look at the light and shadow in the room.

And I do, seeing the dark lines below her shelves,
the curves of slate-grey behind the jugs and delph –
the second, unnoticed room within her kitchen.

Then my eye finds the luminance a wine-glass throws,
an exquisite goblet of shadow and light
cast so casually on the wall.

So often something threadbare about my mind,
I sit at the glass-table by the window,

a sky-bird wings across its surface,
and there's grace in the bird's flight,

grace in the sound of Duffy's cows
not complaint, more like music,

and I can hold off the doctor
telling my girl it's likely to be cancer.

There is a dragonfly on these rivers
which in flight appears bat-black,

but on opening her wings
becomes emerald-green.

I can't help but wonder
if it will be the slurry-runoff that kills her.

Wendell Berry says,
It's hard to be patient in an emergency.

∽

I wake in the night worrying. Money.
My child. My child's health. My child's money.

For a moment I give these problems
back to the One that brought them,
and try to turn instead to praise.

∽

My study this morning smells of the sea
which is some miles off,
but the rain and the open window have
carried its salt-breath inland,
I sit down into it, and am held.

∽

Mid-summer. Grass rippling within me,
I walk in the meadow, unwound,
naming what I see,

foxglove, purple knapweed, thistle, angelica,
honeysuckle, buttercup, heather,

St John's wort, dandelion, plantain,
stitchwort, burnet, clover,

speedwell, valerian, herb Robert,
bird's foot trefoil, purple vetch, wild thyme.

from the long grass
a damselfly lifts on diaphanous wings.

What kind of creatures are we
that all this is not enough?

$\approx$

I took the outstretched hand he offered me
and he received me in my upset and confusion.

$\approx$

Misting rain and the flash of bird-wings in the willows,
the acrobatics of great-tits –
their small carnival of nurture.

From the long grass, the pale harebells
quiet my nagging thoughts,

I try so hard to hear the one within me
delirious with love for the world.

$\approx$

I dream of Vikings, only they are more like Normans
living in a town of cut-stone.

The dream is about war. Because of the fighting,
the Madonna and Child are carried into safe-keeping,

I see her lain down carefully in a vault.
When the war ends, they will bring her home.

Sun reflects off the flowing stream-water,
makes a moving river of light on beech-leaves,
an ease I want to stay in the shelter of,

but this morning I must drive to the city,
must wait while the surgeon
takes a blade to my child's throat.

They have warned us
she may never speak again.

I lean into the light that moves over
the delicate branches,

and try to tame my nervous-system
which is running animal-wild with fear.

Now, Sunlight come with me,
now Beech-leaves stay at my side,
Stream water, flow on through my mind.

I could look up diagrams and X-ray,
but it is enough to be with her bruising,
the inked lines on her livid skin
that we can't yet wash away –
when medicine looks like violence.

But she's back in my hands,
vulnerable as the infant she once was;
everything settling into care,
into the mundane,
and something holy in that.

The sounds of birdsong,
soft rain on the skylight,
through the wall my daughter
laughing on the phone to her friend.

And I can't move from the bed,
so grateful, for the mercies.

⤳

There is less of me this time as we enter the city.
I am insubstantial even to her doctor;

he can look through me and not see
the years I loved her into being,

but it is no hardship now to disappear,
I would pay anything for this news he gives her,
for the light that leaps back into her eyes.

⤳

I mow the grass and afterwards lie
in the hammock, I feel eroded like land worn away.

There's a wind that the willows bow to,
their young branches sough upwards,

the shy belly of each leaf is exposed
and their fragility is a soft silver-green.

I reach down with my toes, knot them
in the grass as if around the feet of a lover.

I try to tell myself the cyst that has grown
in my pelvis has a purpose.

I know it is going to drag me back into fear.
There'll be nights when I wake again with
mortality and the threat of cancer as bedfellows.

Oh pelvis, you've grown a small ocean,
the way our seas are swollen with patches of oil,
the viscous slicks we can't rightly clean,
no matter how much we pretend.

Oh cyst, you're a crystal ball and all I can see
are more doctors and clinical rooms,
the pathos of perishability,
my own and other people's.

If this wind keeps up, these branches
will crack in front of me, and perhaps they must.
Sometimes we do just have to stare
into the face of tragedy.

Now street reveal yourself,
now alleyway appear,
now gate release, now door open.

⁓

I pack for the hospital and try to bring with me
the three Burren hares Mary and I saw at Eagle's rock.

The cliff obscured in cloud until yards from the holy-well,
the sun broke through, and the mist suddenly lifted.

Mary beside me all the long morning
while we waited for the anesthetic.

And afterwards still there, when by some miracle
I am given a small private room off the neon-lit ward,

a quiet lamp, a window of sky
that the seagulls wing across all day.

The night-nurse asks *You don't mind if I*
keep coming back, it's so calm in here,

and I'm reminded of the Handless Maiden
how after she's lost her parents, her home, her hands,
the pear trees in the King's orchard
extend their boughs, offer pears to her lips.

And Dave comes to sit on the hard plastic chair,
making the years of our friendship solid in the room.

And Hannah arrives with fig jam and soft cheese,
a most expensive hospital picnic.

And Ursula drives across two counties
to fetch me home to the shelter of her guest-room,
so by the medicine of friendship I mend.

⤳

Benign. How precious the word becomes –
given to me twice this year.

But nothing in the process benign,
a scouring year.

The gynaecologist reeling off at me hysterectomy,
oophorectomy, salpingectomy, trachelectomy.

My brother confirming that half the women in America
no longer have their wombs.

But I wouldn't sign their form. *My womb
has psycho-spiritual significance*, I said in my paper-gown,

the poor surgeon not knowing where to look.
But he made a promise of a sort.

And if you do have to take it, I'll want it back afterwards,
I said, thinking of a burial in the woods.

No, he says. *It would go to oncology.*
Our body our own until it isn't.

⤳

Home. The willows full of songbirds
so it feels as if I have been sent to a sanitorium
where the treatment is immersion in birdsong.

All day a bird's heart must resonate with song.
I take their notes into my tissue,
absorb their therapy.

Through the kitchen window a glimpse of the sparrow-hawk,
her rare, mythic glide among trees.

Only days since the Zen Centre burned in the California fires,
and the Roshi said the teaching was *impermanence.*

Nothing grows now in the winter garden,
but in the beech tree, raindrops balance on
the tip of each last leaf, a winking diamond of light.

Where the River Inagh curls to meet the sea
a soaring flock of sanderlings,
their white bellies flashing silver.

The world offering reprieve.
And I think this is how it will be from now on,
within the chaos – small, lucid moments.

I line my house with silence, quiet layers settle,
and my thoughts which all year were a blizzard,
begin to drift more gently down.

Every day now is a blessing – and my task
one and the same thing, to re-sacrilise matter,
whether it be the creatures, the land, myself.

To quieten for long enough
to appreciate the spirit within.

A goldfinch comes, balances on a yarrow stalk,
pecks at its last seeds.

Yarrow I set, beneath the orchard I planted.
Not polluted, not drenched in glyphosates.

Beneath the bird's weight, the stalk
curves and bends. The goldfinch lifts free.

Come Nature, help me voice this psalm.
Come Nature, who knows how long either of us has.

in wonder and in grief

Cill Ghrá an Domhain

'We are in the Underworld and haven't figured it out yet. Both inside and outside us. To operate for a second in the Underworld without being annihilated we have to operate from both wonder and grief, at absolutely the same time.'
—Martin Shaw

It's late season, the far end of summer,
just past the equinox, a day of squall,
when finally we take the ferry to the Aran islands.

The wind and ocean so wild, Ursula and I grip
tight the rail, endure the rise and fall and crash of spray,

until Inis Oírr reveals its small harbour of green fields,
grey-stone walls, and soft drifts of rain.

We've been talking of doing this for years. The islands
always out there on our horizon, a trinity of shapes.
So often just three shadows risen from a dark sea

and then on the bright days, the sun glancing
off their cliffs, the light-house rising clear.

But years slipping by where we've let
duty and responsibility get in the way.

The cloud has come in so low, we can hardly see
the lane ahead as Ursula and I cycle out towards
the rust-ruined, run-aground ship her father
photographed her beside when she was a child.

She's speeding on ahead, curving in and out of memory,
while I'm straggling behind among the harebells
and the dwarf blackthorn bushes struggling up out of
the grikes in the rock with their harvest of smoke-blue sloes.

❧

There isn't time to visit Gobnait's chapel
before our ferry sails on for Inis Mór,

but its name follows us, finds me anyway:
Cill Ghrá an Domhain, the church of the love of the world.

Domhain meaning the Earth, and also its people, it's countries and
    wonders.
Domhain also meaning depth, deeply embedded, deeply
    committed.

❧

Of the many things I value Ursula for, most
is how she doesn't judge my mood.
Doesn't diminish, doesn't try to fix.

As friends, we've been companions in wonder
and in grief, the pair of us wearing our century
like a threadbare coat. Balancing on its knife edge, just.

Once, I heard Kay Redfield Jamison say that people who suffer
from depression have less capacity to deny the state of the world.
And I wrote her words down, and kept them close like a charm.

Oh Gobnait, I'll not be denied my love affair with the world,
but like a wounded thing I keep trying to shelter
within briar and thorn. Keep threading grass-stalk and reed,

keep gathering scraps of silver-birch bark and the velvet-soft
stars of beech mast, keep saving small white feathers
to line a fragile nest, only for it all to fray when

on Monday I read of
the heat dome building over America,

on Tuesday, flash-flooding in Germany
has killed 100 people,

on Wednesday, Siberia's fires have released in days
America's entire carbon output for a year,

Thursday brings word of a mysterious
spike in methane levels,

on Friday a third of California's coastal sea-lions
have cancer.

And round it goes again, on Monday I read
the Amazon rainforest emits more carbon than it sequesters.

On Tuesday I hear two million Chinese people
have been displaced by flooding.

On Wednesday I see the floating island of plastic
that drifts perpetually through the Bermuda triangle.

On Thursday I'll be told, on Friday I'll read.
And round it goes again.
Oh Gobnait, you'd weep to see what we've done to your world.

All day the tourists swarm over Dún Aonghasa's
stone amphitheatre like ants in erratic lines of quest,
phones and selfies diminishing the spirits-of-place.

But up on these high cliffs it's clear, we can go no further West.
We have reached the world's end and must turn again,

ours is a crisis of human values, nature's collapse
the manifestation of our mistaken ethics.

Homo sapiens, Homo ecconomicus. We took a wrong turn
and must turn again, evolve: Homo indigene.

With evening the island empties, restores itself.
The last ferry leaves. Something illicit in the way
I climb back up Kilmurvey's hill.

In the stillness of sunset, Dún Aonghasa's stone-temple
has become a wild sanctuary framing endless sea and sky,
a theatre of cloud and light: gold, apricot and charcoal-blue.

The last rays of sun spill a path of liquid gold across
the surface of the ocean. I have no words for such benevolence.

All around me gull cry and beauty.
How limitless it is, our capacity to love.

And nothing more lovely than this journey to the Earth.
The same Earth, I keep saying, as the Medievals saw,

same as the Vikings knew when they named their Gods
for thunder and for spring. Same as Gobnait praised
when she built *Cill Ghrá an Domhain*.

These days I'll tell anyone who'll listen,
about Jung's ideas of *Shadow*.

How it matters so much now that we know
what our culture makes us stow away.

Its shadow letting us deny our harm,
and just as easily subvert any inconvenient emotion.

In the falling twilight I clamber back downhill.
A grey dusk, grey stone descent. Each uneven step

hastening me towards humanity's denouement.
The spell of our narrative nears its end.

The rock-strewn path seems to bookend history,
Bronze-Age Dún Aonghasa at my back,

and across the blackening water, night has already
swallowed the Cailleach's hills, Hag's Head
and the Burren with its ancient sacred caves.

Caves so dark the other senses compensate for blindness,
hearing becomes acute, touch a small rapture.

Caves of sparse relic and votive offering: antler,
oyster shell, amber rings from the Baltic sea,
a wolf's tooth pierced and worn as a totem at the neck.

I carry them, or they carry me over the stumbling rocks –
something like faith – as I head on into the falling night.

⁀

Gobnait, if I could do anything at all, I'd brave my arm
into our dark, the way prehistoric women once put their hands
into the bees-nest bole of trees to draw out honey.

So help me Gobnait. All that's left to us now,
is to pull from our *shadow* our fierce love for the world,
lá dheireadh an domhain – until the end of time.

www.ingramcontent.com/pod-product-compliance
Lightning Source LLC
LaVergne TN
LVHW091228080426
835509LV00009B/1211